Covenant Pathway To Parental Blessing

DR A. J. AJENGBE

DEDICATION

To God Almighty.

CONTENTS

ACKNOWLEDGMENTS

My appreciations go to everyone who made this work a success.

Preface

Many people Struggle in life, doing so much to make ends meet, yet to no avail. They look for solutions from various quarters. Some consult books; they could be termed epitome of knowledge. Some even become highly religious, worship God fervently, went through various deliverance programs in anticipation that there problems would be solved and would soon be living in affluence, but all to no avail.

Unfortunately, what some of these people failed to realize is that such miserable life could be as a result of lack of parental blessings from their parents or guardian as they grew up systematically in life.

This is why this book is been orchestrated your way this moment, to correct every hindrance you've been experiencing in life due to the hands of blessings withheld over your life from your parents or guardians.

This book will reveal to you the wisdom of having parental blessings released over your life, and guide you on how to amend your ways and claim these special blessings that mattered greatly.

Chapter 1

What Is Parental Blessing

Before we examine what is parental blessing let's find out who a parent is?

A parent is the father or mother of an offspring meaning the parents' reproduce the offspring. They may be biological or spiritual.

What about parents?

- They share their chromosome with the offspring which contain the DNA of the father meaning you are a continuation of the existence of your parents.
- From the womb the mother provides protection, food, nutrients and blood for the child. The blood in the body of the child is principally your father's blood.
- The cells in your body are your parents.
- Parents are caregivers especially the father being a provider and your mother being a care giver. Your parents are your first destiny helpers.

- Your parents normally have more understanding of you because they know you more than you.
- You will either look like your parents, grandparents or their family members, that's not your choice to make.

We now look at parental blessing

Parental blessing are destiny verdicts issued by a parent on a child. In order of hierarchy after God, your parents come next. It doesn't not matter if they are behaving the way you want or not, if they bless you; you are blessed and if they do otherwise no prayer can help you.

Abraham didn't bless Isaac so God had to bless him again with the blessing of his father but Isaac didn't make the mistake he blessed his sons (Genesis 27: 27-29, 40) Jacob demonstrated the very well he prophesied on his children (Genesis 49; 3-27)

Parental blessing is the blessing of your parent over your life and destiny. They are words but they are not just mere words but destiny pictures released for fulfillment in a man's life.

The man of God over your life is your spiritual parent. That's why not just everyman should have authority over you. You need to do a soul searching to locate the rightful man. Remember that your spiritual parents don't need you likewise you biological parents but you need them for everything. Tell me how much you can pay to your parents for upbringing. You will discover you can't, you may only show appreciation. Even if you are a professor today, imagine if you didn't survive the first three months of you didn't go to primary school how will you become a director, Engineer, professor today.

Parental blessings could be a silent wish by your parent to make you succeed. These are not words but parents' heart being with you.

What is parental blessing?

- Wellness in life: these are so many people that it's not well with today because their parents have issued a curse or has not blessed them.
- Long life: if you want to live long and escape the premature death ravaging this generation then collect all that God loaded in your parents in term of blessing.
- Divine favor: you enjoy sweatless favor as a blessed man by your parents.
- Divine Rain: you enjoy refreshing as you engage tirelessly in blessing your parents.
- Divine protection:

- Supernatural Speed;
- Pacesetter of destiny: their words today create your tomorrow.
- Prevail against Foes:
- Divine Help
- Supernatural strength
- Fruitfulness; any form of unfruitfulness can be terminated by parental blessing
- Overflowing blessing
- Divine enthronement and crowning: see Genesis 50: 3 a whole nation mourning Jacob for 70 days because he has a worthy son. I pray for you: God will bless your children so that nations will declare one whole year work free for your investment in your children. In Egypt, nobody knows Jacob it was Joseph. May the honor of your children rub off on you.
- Supernatural prosperity: genesis 49: 11
- Headship, leadership, first-all-the-time Genesis 49: 8

Parental blessings refers to positive forces that follow you and bring you good luck due positive words spoke forth over your life by those with parental authority over you. Some people refer to these guardian ancestors, angels, spirits etc. Maybe you want to ask who has parental authority. It is any person who has parental relationship with you, whether biological or otherwise, though some people do not know their biological parents, mostly in black society. Some people lose their biological parents at a tender age. This is why parental authority does not have to do only with who carried you in her womb for whole nine months. You may still have one or both of your biological parents. Some people have parents who are bad role models while some people are blessed with good character parents.

I believe parents have major role and contributions to what their children become later in life. Whether positive or negative role; this depends on the guardian or parent in question. The major point is to strengthen the encouraging influence of parental authority in our lives so as to face situations courageously. This positive influence should be through blessings that our guardians and parents pronounce into our lives, not that people should not struggle in life if they carry parental blessings. It is mandatory that children get parental blessings since it helps them cope especially when things are actually difficult in life.

Evidence or lack of parental blessings

The confirmation of parental blessing is that whenever you endeavor things in life, they fall in space with comparative ease as contrasting to others. However, there are people who are really struggling in life.

Again, parental blessings are the good fate and farewell wishes that accompany children in life. These are the great wishes that appear from the depths of the hearts of people who have authority over your life. The proof of such blessings is made manifest in a variety of forms. These blessings can be associated with relationships, schooling, professional life, property, businesses, etc.

Relationships

Relationships are one area that people will hardly believe that parental blessings affect greatly. Indeed, parental blessings affect every area of our lives, as well as relationships.

Parental blessings might help you select person that truly loves and care about you. You may make some mistakes in choosing partner. Even at that, the presence of your parental well wishes will enable you come out of bad relationships fairly unhurt. We all know bad relationships hurt. Sad to say, some people lose their lives in terrible relationships, meaning their way out is the coffin.

Parental blessings can also help you connect with right people who will assist you to make progress in life. The truth is that some people are doing well in life due to the wonderful relationships they had with awesome people. You may want to think about those people who have contributed greatly to your success, and get a clearer picture.

Professional life

Unemployment abounds in every nation. Every country struggles with this issue. Circumstances like these call for parental blessings. Such blessings will help you find the right job and progress needed. Parental blessings can help you unlock the doors to the promotion you really deserve. If one doesn't have these blessings in life, he can do everything right but still be unseen for promotion.

Business

Parental blessings can help you get your business plan rightly approved, land that required tender and be able to carry on and grow that business of yours further. Sometimes, some people get such tenders, experience overnight success suddenly to wither and disappear into forgetfulness in months or years later. Therefore, you need to acquire these blessings on a nonstop basis; then you will leave a legacy of success.

What are the conditions?

Parental blessings have conditions for implementation. First-born children usually automatically meet the criteria for the blessings, although they still need to access them via the keys I've mentioned above. As for other children, they have to access their own blessings gradually as they grow up. However, there are pre-conditions for the blessings to be unlocked and occur in one's life.

- **Sincerity**

Sincerity is paramount for accessing parental blessings. You must have a sincere and clean heart. The acts of kindness and gifts must be carried out from a willing heart so that this will not become a operation where the child does his parents a help out of self-centered ambitions.

- **Spoken words**

There is need for guardian or parent to be uttering words of blessings over the child's life. It is for this basis that you have to unlock these things personally. Endeavour to physical present gift or show acts of kindness to them as this will test your love and affection for your parent.

Chapter 2

How To Connect With Parental Blessings

How to access parental blessings

Having known what parental blessings are, how then do you access them? For some people, it could be easy for them to access these blessings because their biological parents are still alive and are readily reached. Some will find it tough to access the blessings since they do not have fine relations with their parents. You can access your parental blessings by loving your parents and appreciating them. You need to do things, tangible and intangible for them, and live a lifestyle that will make your parents be proud of you. You cannot have parental blessings if the people who have parental authority over you are sad with you. Below are the keys you can use to unlock your parental blessings.

Gifts

One way to unlock this kind of blessings is by giving gifts to your parents or guardians. These can be anything that you identify they need and will be glad about. There is no boundary to the gifts you should give them. You know them much better than anyone out there. Choose the gift and hand it over to them in person so that you can perceive the joy in their face and wait for the words of gratitude and blessings from them. Don't wait for special events like Christmas, birthdays, Easter, etc. Every time is appropriate to access your parental blessings. Hence, you should make it a regular habit to do in whole-hearted manner. These wonderful gifts can help greatly to unlock the hidden treasures locked inside your parents for you.

Acts of kindness

To access parental blessings, you can also do something for your parents like cooking for them or cleaning, these will make them happy. There is no limit regarding the ways you should help your parents despite not giving them material thing. They will be joyful and bless you for that. Think of those talents and knowledge you have that can be of great benefits to your parents. You can follow them to shops, bank, etc. It is these caring that will prompt them to bless you.

1. Eat: Genesis 27:9 … eat… bless let your parent be in your budget. You can't be eating fine things and give trash to your parents. They must eat your money, wear your clothes, live in your house, go on trips abroad at your expense. You will wonder why Isaac said' give me venison to eat. There is a connection between the heart and the mouth. Just as the mouth is the gateway of the body. The heart is the gateway to the soul.

2. Obedience Ephesian 6:1. The Bible said when you obey your parents you are doing what is right and you cannot be doing what is right and go wrong in life. Total obedience is key to miracles. Don't say they are old fashioned obey their words to the later. Thought you may not understand now but you will understand.

3. Honor them Ephesians 6:2

What is honor?

Honor means to have value, decoration, preference. There are people whose parents don't have value in their eyes. No wonder they are on a steady fall in life. Reference your parents. See them like God. In the actual fact they are your earthly God.

4. Serve your parents 2 kings 3: 11b. This is Elisha, but his CV was not a powerful prophet who divided Jordan but "… who poured water on the hands of Elijah". If you don't serve your parents your children will not serve you! Visit them, wash them cloths, make their hair, if they are too old bath them and collect your generation blessing from their mouth.

In Christendom these days there are many who do not want to serve they just want to become General

Overseer over night. Sorry, personally if I don't know your spiritual fathers and I can't attend a church just because you can see vision or prophesy doesn't make a man of God. Without fathers you don't have feathers to fly said r D K Olukoya.

5. Observe your parents; I grew up to see my Dad according people due respect even to his own children then I follow suite. I read in Gods servant Bishop Oyedepo's book that by 11pm he tell his staff goodnight and good morning to Jesus that how my adventure into midnight prayers and praises started everyday for eight years.

The opposite of parental blessings is parental curses. If you have done anything that earned you parent curses before then the only remedy I know is to seek the forgiveness and blessing of your parents but if they are deed then you need serious prayer and deliverance.

Parental curses can

- It limits potential Genesis 49: 4
- It attract other curses of life
- It leads to division
- Spiritual and physical barrenness
- Demotion of all sorts
- Breakdown instead of breakthroughs

- No helpers
- Misfired aggression
- Resistance in the place of enthronement
- Spoiling the spoiler

Importance of Parental Blessing

The Bible advises that children should obey their parents. It says that in the Lord, this is right and in all things, for this is much pleasing to the Lord. This also go hand-in-hand with the Lord's Commandment in Exodus: honor your father and your mother, that your days may be long in the land which Lord your God has given you.

The major key to societal stability is honor and respect for one's parents and their authority. The book of Ephesians says, Child in the home should be voluntarily under the authority of his parents with obedient and submission to them as the agents of the Lord so placed over him, obeying their parents as if obeying God Himself. The book of Colossians says the only restriction to a child's obedience is if parents demand from them something contrary to God's Word.

It makes great sense to honor your parents and obey them. They are part of your life as long as they and you are alive. Hopefully too, they will be grandparents of your children.

Chapter 3

Parental Blessings And Your Battles

Isaiah 65:8

Haven known what parental blessing is then what is Battle?

A battle is warfare, it's a fight. It is a force that seeks to resist a bloodline. If it conquered your parent then you can't escape expect you fight. It is the battle of the fathers and your mother house; it is a battle with the following characteristics:

- Saying no to your destiny voice or permanent silences
- Calling you from your destiny headship to the tail region
- Seeking to kill your glory
- Seeking to shut down your start
- Burying your virtues
- Posing limits and limitations, stagnation, and backwardness to a man's journey
- Hindering your head from attaining fame and fortune

- Wants you to be like your father or not exceed your fathers
- They normally have heavy influence of witchcraft and bewitchment
- Divination and scorey become prevalent
- Thick darkness beclouds a man's destiny
- A man shedding tears in the midst of plenty
- Continual and perpetual failure and defeat
- Favour is scare or not available at all
- Misfired aggression and hatred
- Collective captivity is visible: everybody is poor, everybody is barren
- The first is becoming the last
- A man of wisdom is not noticed
- A jewel in dustbin
- A captor becoming a captive
- A man become a shadow of his real self

Battles are real. Victory is also real. It is my prayer that you will win your battle. Because in life it is warfare before fun fair. Parental blessing may be a voice speaking against your battle. It doesn't matter even if you are far away. Battles can locate a believer and unbeliever alike. According to Isaiah 65:8 that voce was speaking destroy it not for there is a blessing in it. The blessing makes you indestructible. The blessing makes you unassaultable. The blessing confers on you dignity and honor.

Who are those in battle?

- Christians who are under evil pattern in the lineage
- Those going through unpleasant situation and need divine intervention
- Those living a single life without their divine spouse
- Those who want to be gainfully employed against the wish of household enemies
- Those who have not conceived and want to conceive by fire by force
- Those under constant threat and conspiracy of human in their lives
- Marriage gone scour
- Disease and infirmities that have defiles medical condition
- Those being pursued by enemies
- Those operation under the manner of curses, be it generational, ancestral, parental, environmental
- Those with heavy burden and satanic yokes
- Anybody experiencing unexplainable joblessness

- Those who mare confused about life and re lacking direction generally
- Those who experience marital crisis
- All those doing profitable hard jobs

Chapter 4

Transference Of Virtue Of Parental Blessing

I encourage parents to have 5 minutes of parental blessing daily on their children. This is different from prayer its declaration to shape their destiny. Don't wait till you are old-time like Jacob, keep releasing them

We see an interesting story in 2 kings 2: 1-15. This was Elisha pursing something in Elijah. The other children of the prophet were mocking him. Your other siblings may be mocking you but continue. Later he collected the mantle and they bow their kneels.

What interest me most is that said 'his master will be taken away from your head" why the head? Parental blessings is a covering of your head meaning your destiny. What a parent your head is coverless

Before we look at virtues of parental blessing; we shall consider what happens when people don't have parents physically and spiritually

- You fen d for yourself
- No parental care, advise and direction

- No affection
- Deprivation of food
- Chances of survival is slim
- We are doing this to access the impact of parenting biologically. Psychologically and spiritually

Spiritually, without parenting you don't have a destiny. No matter how anointed you are someone somewhere has been prepared to bring out your potentials and fan it to fame. You will need mentoring, discipleship, followership for the ol of your father to rub on you. The anointing is real. The power of God exists bit there are levels of empowerment that is largely transferred

Bishop oyedepo will always talk about his experience how he prayed for the oil of Hagin and allowed till it dropped on him

How do you know your mentor?

- There is s a soul tie
- Careful search
- Pray about it

What is in parental blessings?

- Divine favor

- Wellness in life
- Long life
- Divine rain
- Divine protection
- Supernatural speed
- Pacesetter of destiny
- Prevail against foes
- Divine help
- Supernatural strength
- Fruitfulness
- Overflowing blessing
- Divine enthronement
- Supernatural prosperity
- Headship leadership all the time

DR A. J. AJENGBE

About The Author

Dr A. J. Ajengbe is the GMD/CEO of Ajengbe Group a conglomerate that comprises: Jengbens Global Concept limited, Pearls Associates Financial services, Ajengbe Publications, Global Mission education Centre and Sunday Emmanuel Ajengbe Memorial Foundation.